Maps and Globes

by Ellen Bari

Libby C. Booth Elementary

PEARSON

Scott
Foresman

Editorial Offices: Glenview, Illinois • Parsippany, New Jersey • New York, New York
Sales Offices: Needham, Massachusetts • Duluth, Georgia • Glenview, Illinois
Coppell, Texas • Ontario, California • Mesa, Arizona

A globe shows Earth. Globes are shaped like
Earth. They are round like a ball. They let
you see the whole world.

Maps are drawings of Earth. They take our round Earth and put it on flat paper. Maps can be folded. They are easier to carry than globes.

This park has many **mountains** and is covered with forests. Mountains are the highest kind of land. Forests are large areas with many trees and plants.

There are some green parts on this map. Green shows that there are many forests. You can use color to help you read a map.

This is a photograph of a beach. The water is the **ocean**. An ocean is very large. It is made of salt water.

In this photograph it is easy to see where the land ends and the ocean begins.

Remember that globes use color to show what things are. Blue is the color used to show oceans, **rivers**, and lakes. By looking at the globe, you can see where the blue water is.

Glossary

mountain the highest kind of land

ocean a very large body of salt water

river a long body of water which usually
moves toward a lake or the ocean

Write to It!

If you were going on a trip with your family, would you bring a map or globe? Why? Write two sentences about your choice.

Write your sentences on another sheet of paper.

Libby C. Booth Elementary

Every effort has been made to secure permission and provide appropriate credit for photographic material. The publisher deeply regrets any omission and pledges to correct errors called to its attention in subsequent editions.

Unless otherwise acknowledged, all photographs are the property of Scott Foresman, a division of Pearson Education.

Photo locators denoted as follows: Top (T), Center (C), Bottom (B), Left (L), Right (R), Background (Bkgd)

Opener: Getty Images; 1 Getty Images; 2 Getty Images; 3 Getty Images; 4 Getty Images; 5 Map Resources; 6 Corbis Media; 7 Getty Images; 8 Corbis Media

Fun Facts

- The oldest maps are more than three thousand years old.

- Six hundred years ago many people believed the world was flat.

- There are more mountains under the ocean than on dry land.

Genre	Comprehension Skill	Text Features
Nonfiction	Find the Main Idea	• Glossary • Maps • Globe

Scott Foresman Social Studies

PEARSON

Scott
Foresman

scottforesman.com

ISBN 0-328-14799-0

90000

9 780328 147991